Not Enough:

Musings on Grief

A collection of
original poetry by
Bruce Marshall Sterling

Stage 3 Press
Boulder, Colorado

Not Enough: Musings on Grief

BruceSterlingLLC.com
Stage 3 Press Boulder, CO

Second paperback edition 2022
ISBN 9781736561102 (paperback)

Dedication

This book is dedicated to my parents, Fred and Hilda Sterling, who continue to teach and guide me, even after their passing. They've led me on this journey of rawness, vulnerability, compassion and gratitude; now expressed through poetry.

It was the passing of longtime family friend Alma Rosenberg that inspired the poem and book title, Not Enough. Conversely, our love was more than enough.

This book is also dedicated to you, the reader, who has suffered through sadness, loss and grief which brought you to these pages. May the words which follow bring you comfort or at least a recognition there is a community of us who understand, empathize and support you through this dark path to a more compassionate life.

Table of Contents

Preface

It was the evening of my 56th birthday when two police officers came to the door. The words, "There's no easy way to say this" as they entered the living room, caused my brain to shuffle scenarios; none of which made sense. In the moments that followed I was launched into a different reality from which I'll never return. My parents died earlier that day and my familiarity with grief went from 0 to 60 in 7 words.

In the years that followed I found grief to be a profound tool to unravel my own previously repressed feelings. It's also a bridge that connects me to other people more intimately. We're open and vulnerable when grieving, especially if someone talks to us with compassion and presence.

Feelings are heavy when loss is in one's heart. Most people avoid talking with those who are grieving, yet it can be very helpful. It's a difficult path that knows no straight road. If you're willing to be there with those in this state, there's often no need to do much more than listen.

Initially my inspiration for writing about grief came from my own experience. Later, I wrote poems to friends and acquaintances who were suffering from loss. I've included both in this book.

As I think about those who are grieving I settle into the creative process with a depth and compassion that always flows beneath the surface ever waiting to be expressed. I consider that a privilege and hope the words in this book offer solace, inspiration and understanding during trying times.

For true healing we need to be patient, act with compassion and forgiveness, and ultimately be more humane, with ourselves and others.

Grief is an integrating process. As we integrate these strong feelings, we impact our world at large. Loss and grief help us to see our commonality. They're part of being human, and humanity is our bond.

Foreword

As an author and a friend, Bruce's Musings on Grief holds a very special place in my heart. We met in a class some years ago and bonded over time regarding our experiences with grief. His with the sudden loss of his parents and mine with the long and painful illness and loss of my daughter, Cristina. It's very comforting to have people to talk to openly about grief. Bruce is one of those people.

He has taken his heartfelt energy and compassion and written this collection of poetry. It comes from feelings that reflect his and others' experience of loss and the grief that accompanies it.
Madeline Goldstein, Author
Love In Action. My Daughter's Battle with Cancer A Mother's Memoir

I Have an Affection
for Grief

Those grieving

are deep in emotion,

deep in their personal truth

and

they are extraordinarily present.

Looking into the eyes

of someone who is grieving

is a gift

that few offer.

It's a skill of mine.

I did the coursework.

Family Photos

I compulsively photographed

the scene;

the barely scarred pole,

the stop sign that didn't,

the tree that did.

Looking at the photos

you'd ask

"How could anyone

live through that?"

They didn't.

Part 1 – Confusion

Twice Born

We are born once
through the dark canal
of mother
into all that life may offer.

We are born yet again
through the dark canal
of grief
back into life
with all that death has taken.

Longings

Longing,
longing to be,
longing to be again,
to be whole
without the hole
so deep
the wishing well
can't hear the wishes.

Peace Lies in Surrender

What strife
to look
for those who've passed
with eyes
that see a solid world.

Loss brings more struggle than
you can bear,
more pain than
a heart should feel.

Mourn, my child,
for what was yours,
for that which will not be;
promises stolen,
life not lived
and love cut short for thee.

Surrender into
what you had
for all it was,
and is.

Breathe it deeper,
feel it tender
and cry
your pool of tears.

You never saw it coming.

In life's due course,
we see most clearly
in reverse.

A Pairing of Pairs

Part 1

Most lessons are straightforward
though it may take a long time
for repercussions
to come full circle,
for effect to mirror cause.

They are but one package
traveling in pairs.
There is no cause without effect
nor effect without its cause
because
the universe is like that.

Part 2

Grief and love are twin comets
speeding through the universe
winding back and forth
their flight inextricably connected
until they are no more.
Only
grief is slow
and the path is unpredictable

and the universe is your heart
and the comet is you
and the winding back and forth
is nature's way
of teaching you
the hard parts of love,
like a rock tumbler
smoothing your rough edges
until worn down,
and polished,
like the gem you must become.

Comets dancing through space
with enough distance to
avert collision
and destruction
but enough proximity
that love is held captive by grief
and grief deepens love.

This emotional dance,
this cosmic dance,
takes us for the ride of a lifetime
and there's no getting off.

It's that personal.

Collapsing Worlds

Life and death
a clash of paradoxes
and grief stands between them both
like Hercules' mighty arms
holding apart collapsing worlds.
Sweat on his furrowed brow
can be easily mistaken
for heartache and tears.

The strain on his face
resembles what you see
when you dare glance at a mirror.

Wrenching emotions
stare back.
Feelings of love, tragedy,
and nostalgia
sit encapsulated
in your heart and soul.

Push desperately
against the collapsing worlds;
your conflicting efforts,
not wanting to be set free
for fear of flying apart
into nothingness.

For what is left
when nothing is left?

Living in Grief

The years drag
slowly
like razor blades
through heart chambers.

Pain
with each breath
and the beat, beat, beat
that tells you
you're still alive
while dying inside.

Intermission

This is hard. There's no doubt about it. Don't feel the need to take in more than your heart can tolerate.

Read as you wish, take a break, breathe, cry, go for a walk. Be patient with yourself. You don't own the process. It owns you regardless of your strength and will. You're human and there's no perfection in that. Don't try to get over it. You have ever changed. While more painful than you've imagined, the transmutation will become your super power. You may sit in doubt now because you can only know it in retrospect.

Part 2 – Community

Grief Haiku #1

Grief is intimate.
It pulls on heartstrings so deep.
Rips us more human.

The Story

My mother played piano
all through her life.
Literally.
Starting at 3,
performing at 4,
stopping on
my 56th birthday.

But she didn't stop for me,
she didn't stop for her music.
She stopped
for the utility pole
that crushed
the car she was driving.
The car my father,
the other passenger,
bought.

Bought,
because they're so dependable,
so reliable
but with an Achilles heel,
a Trojan horse,
a death trap.

The throttle control sensor
whose inconvenient truth
happened to stick
causing an acceleration that
regardless of her
desperate attempt to steer
into a Big Lots big lot
and damn near succeeded,
only not.

Destiny called, no,
destiny commanded
and launched them,
my bloodline,
into instant death for her.
He, airlifted,
left his body within
the hour.

2000 miles away,
at the time of impact,
I was opening
the birthday card
she sent
days before.

The timing still ironic.

6 hours later,
heading to my birthday dinner,
knock, knock.
Hi officers,
c'mon in.
"There's no easy way to say this."
A short sentence.
A death sentence.
All words understandable
yet the pictures unfolded
like playing cards
shuffled upside down.
My normally
slow paced brain
ran through
scenario after scenario
in godless Godspeed
and came back to the only one
that was obviously true.
A short sentence,
the sentence of a lifetime
with a lifetime sentence.

Anything About Music

She took to the piano.
I don't know why.
By the time I emerged
from her body
20 years had passed.

Perfect pitch made her a natural,
that,
and her penchant for taking
charge,
and her love of performing.
Not a lot of self-esteem,
but enough.
Around a piano,
she was beyond bold.
The instrument was her friend
and any nearby ears
were her audience.
It was also her in-road
to any organization that was open.
It was her in-road
to any community
that would appreciate her.
And they did.

School plays, synagogues, cruise
ships, retirement centers,
which, by the way,
is where she was headed
when the car malfunctioned.
She was absolutely heroic
and damn lucky
in avoiding all people and
vehicles
but not the utility pole,
where her luck ended.

Her swan song was
the screeching of tires.

The Club

I never
want anyone
to go through a loss
that brings them to grief.

Yet,
I never
want to deprive anyone
from the miracles,
blessings
and depth that result.

They're hard won
and profoundly bittersweet.
It's a painfully curious pairing
and
wholly transformative.

Yes, my friend,
the dues for membership
are varied
but none of us escape the club.

Who knows,
maybe it's the prerequisite
for what lies beyond.

The Depths of Humanity

Grief is
a powerfully connecting bridge
for those left behind.
It pulls us
to the cliffs of vulnerability
and pushes us
into the depths of humanity.

Meet Me on the Field

Loss is universal,
grief specific.
My parents
instantly gone upon impact.
I know that loss.

A mother watched and fought for
decades
as medicine failed her beloved
daughter.
A father missing his son
taken a lifetime ago
yet still resides in his heart and
soul.
A classmate's brother
pruned as the tree was nearing
his prime.

Loss levels the field
and who shows up
brings their story,
their humanity,
the pieces of their heart
wanting in vain
to *peace* back together
as if it could be one yet again.

Though each knows
the cracks and tears
have seams made of feelings
ever raw
never to be healed.

We all end up upon this field,
never by choice.

Our assignment:
find ourselves
within the remnants,
find compassion
for ourselves and our field-mates
for therein lies
our hope,
our soul,
our peace.

Inside the Boxing Match

An acquaintance of mine constructed an art / performance exhibit designed to help people process grief around death.

The exhibit was housed in a storage unit. Donors provided a small number of items that were placed in individual cardboard boxes for viewing. The viewer entered the storage unit and observed the contents while listening to a recording of donors explaining the items and why they selected those pieces. A chair was also in the space for participants to sit and process their thoughts, feelings and emotions as they surfaced.

I participated as a donor and spectator.

The Boxing Match

Here I sit
in a box.

A metal box
filled with
cardboard boxes,
cardboard boxes
filled with
personal treasures,
meaningless relics,
living touchstones;
touching through the veil
into emptiness.

Peering into boxes,
feeling into lives,
feeling into death
and the gap between -
through stories imagined
and my own remembered.

My stories,
of a lifetime ago,
actually 4 lifetimes,
starting when we were a family
building foundations
before they cracked
and I fell through
into someone else's reality.

A lifetime later
scaling the finger holds in the
foundation
I pull myself out
and walk back into life.

Dredging the past
with today's insights
shifts life's wobbly limp
to a mindful gait.

"If I only knew then what I know
now..."

Looking backward is invaluable
when it teaches you
how to move forward.

Grief's Accomplice

Time,
measured by years or months
now measured in moments,
breaths
and beats.

Time,
not the touted healer of wounds.
Memories are cellular,
alive inside us
not photographs fading
in the light of day
or in storage
with relics and symbols.
Memories keep them alive
and keep us alive
with a newfound
profound presence
known only
outside of time.

Love Doesn't Die

There are no words.
The feeling is deep
and dark
and painful.

Still,
from there
extraordinary love ferments
and fertilizes compassion
and the immediacy of life.

The richness of that soil,
through decay and suffering,
spurs life on
with connections
you can now make
with authenticity.

Love doesn't die
but loss tears us apart.
It rips us into raw,
unadulterated humanity,
the depth of which
we usually
just graze the surface.

Like a cold creek plunge
on a sultry summer's day,
the shock on hot skin
stripping complacency
until we become
the new balance of
invigorated awareness,
seeing life clearly
with all its fullness.

Questions remain for years,
answers trickle in over time
and for some not at all.

Being at peace
with loss like this
is refining
and in return
bestows
the perspective of a saint.

Wishing you much solace
my friend.

The Persistent Blindsiding
by Grief

Deep and agonizing
bloodless wounds
fresh and raw
new or
new yet again
leaving you
filled with questions.

Questions answered over time,
questions never answered.

Lonely,
regardless of company,
regardless of your support.

Regardless,
find a few confidants
that can hold space
for your ups and downs,
your criss crosses
that barge in
with a forged invitation

disguised
as a smell,
a word,
a song,
a thought that comes
from nowhere
and slaps you
with emotions
designed to
tear you open,
tear you larger,
tear you into humanity
that can forge bonds
with a total stranger
from overheard words
of pain or sorrow.

Find a confidant,
someone,
someone compassionate,
someone undaunted by tears,
someone who can be patient,
who can be quiet,
or maybe utter

one
heartfelt
word.

You're strong,
you're amazing and
you're human.

As I told myself
too many short years ago,
if there's anytime
to cut myself a break,
this is it.

Much compassion to you
and may grace
be your steadfast companion.

Part 3 - Integration

Grief Haiku #2

Stillness, emptiness
allow the soul to expand.
Grief, a strange ally.

Dancing Through Grief

Grief is a dance,
not particularly genteel.
It has its way with you
with spins and turns
unannounced.

If lucky
you can keep time
but you never keep up.

A smell, a sound, or
an errant thought
becomes an open door
for the bull's entrance
to your sacred China shop.

The waves of intensity
surprise even you
as tears spontaneously take leave
mid-sentence.

There is no strategy
or realistic defense,
merely faith, surrender and grace
whenever and however
they may appear.

Time may soothe
but only in retrospect.

There is no cure
yet you will endure.

Diamonds and Butterflies

The path you've been wrought is
the nature and whim of grief.
This upper level course of life
adds the color, cut and clarity
of the diamond qualities
a human exemplifies
when becoming an awakened,
compassionate soul.

The heat and pressure
of earth-forces
are not more nor less than
the heartache of Hades,
the anguish of Shiva
and the process of Shakti.

Butterflies make
the metamorphosis
of the caterpillar
seem worthwhile
but the alchemical process
within the cocoon
is hidden through
transformational stages
unbelievable to the human mind.

The grieving understand
the nuances too well.

Mourn the person you were
as you leave the cocoon behind.

One never celebrates
the colors and patterns
of ones own wings,
but others
see your majesty
and understand
the true meaning
of awe.

Miracles Abide There

We each have loss,
none escape it.

Grief,
the healing process
that reintegrates
feelings and thoughts,
desires and regrets,
the past and
no future.

Through life,
through living
we choose the palette
but never
the timing,
the circumstances or
the outcome.

So there it is,
shock,
then sadness,
later
reality,
an unreal reality
the likes of which
you've never experienced.

Like taffy,
you're pulled
into shapes
that leave you
in a state
from which you can never return.

Like flying in clouds
you can't tell which end is up
even when firmly planted
in your seat.

Like walking the streets
Christmas morning
when gifts are exchanged
and no one's outside.

Like you've walked into
the emotional post-apocalypse.

Like love has filled your heart
but the drain plug
is three times the size
it should be,
and the vacuum left
collapses
everything
that made sense,
everything
that gave you substance,
everything.

Grief,
the humanizing,
humbling
shape-shifter
that tears
the fabric of you
and explodes your heart
into newer dimensions
you didn't realize
you signed up for.

I don't wish the pain on anybody
I just know the value of the
outcome.

Miracles abide there,
if you can just see.

The Great Equalizer

Grief knocks on
the door
of humanity,
the door
of mortality,
the door
of eternity.
Never desired,
rarely welcomed,
always heart tearing,
heart-opening,
devastating
and the great educator
of how big we need to be.

Grief bridges
from one soul to another
because the depths
rarely plumbed
are shared in confidence.
It's a connector like no other.

The common feeling,
that common emotion
makes us look
beyond the shallow,
past the veneer,
through the veil,
into our divinity,
the conduit
from one human being to
another.

Grief is
the great equalizer.

Rapids

Whitewater's rapids
so named
because of the fast moving
current
over which you travel.

The rapids of grief
are slow moving
yet equally tumultuous.

Fast or slow is relative
yet
time brings grace
and grace brings forgiveness,
compassion and breath.
Breath returns slowly
when you've stopped holding it
like the dreams vacant from your
cupped hands.

Like the lessons of the river,
the ever-changing landscape
and journey of grief
teaches us about life,
depth,
and our own passing.

We cannot hold it at bay,
hide from it,
or in reality, deny it.

While being at its effect is
disempowering,
surfing the wave,
with patience, presence
and hope
is our greatest salvation.

Not Enough

Words mean nothing
when a loss is so close.
Good intentions
don't undo
losing the
days gone by
and the ones never to be.
Hearts break
but love is not lost.
Condolences don't console.
Your pain is un-grounding,
no place to land.
You're un-tethered
in space,
dark, cold and unfamiliar
never wanting it to be familiar.

But words,
good intentions and condolences
are all we have
to show our love,
to reveal our inability
to erase your suffering,
to ease the darkness
that takes the color
out of life.

It's the best we can do
and it's not enough.

Cristina

You came here to learn
on a hurried timeline,
and so you did
even with the handicaps of
poor health
and poorer health care.

You were protected by
a mother's love;
buffered
and supported
with more love and joy
than most are given.
Laughter and love
were your sword and shield,
yours to brandish
in a moment's notice.
A smile, a phrase, or
a stern word when others needed
correcting;
you held court.

Natural leader,
even before your rigorous
training
raised you to a powerhouse
few saw
but all knew.

Kindness and beauty
were the cloak of the fighter.
Respect was duly accorded
for those that knew your
suffering
also knew your strength.

You were taken too soon
from friends and family.
Your new assignment
beyond this plane,
a dimension unknown to mortals,
yet you leak messages
through one person or another
like the movie Michael -
say this, but only when I tell you.

You drizzle blessings
on a schedule
only you understand.
They keep your loved ones
on their toes
even when hope is lost
or misplaced.

Your reminder comes through
like the reverberations
of a gong strike,
"pay attention,
I'm here."

And so you are.

Acknowledgments

I want to thank my good friend, editor, writing coach and leader by example, Madeline Goldstein. Her gentle suggestions and constant encouragement made this book possible.

Special thanks to my friend and exquisite photographer, David Hoadley, for the author's photo and additional work on the book's cover.

My deep gratitude to all those who shared stories of their lives and became the inspiration for many of the poems in the book. We have been broken open. May wisdom, humility, serenity and compassion be the gifts you glean for the pain of loss.

Thanks to Cristina who leads me to the next step, and the next, with just a hint at the future.

www.ingramcontent.com/pod-product-compliance
Lightning Source LLC
Chambersburg PA
CBHW072027060426
42449CB00035B/3002